STOP and LOOK
ILLUSIONS

Written by Robyn Supraner
Illustrated by Renzo Barto

Troll Associates

Library of Congress Cataloging in Publication Data

Supraner, Robyn.
  Stop and look.

  SUMMARY: Presents optical illusions, some of which
the reader constructs himself, showing relative sizes,
color changes, and patterns that play tricks on one's
eyes. Includes explanations of the illusions.
    1. Optical illusions—Juvenile literature.
[1. Optical illusions] I. Barto, Renzo. II. Title.
QP495.S96   152.1'48   80-23799
ISBN 0-89375-434-X (case)
ISBN 0-89375-435-8 (pbk.)

CONTENTS

WHICH IS BIGGER?

An illusion is a kind of trick. When your eyes play tricks on you, it is called an *optical illusion.* Should you believe everything you see? Before you answer, try these experiments!

Here's what you need:

White paper

Compass

Scissors

Pencil

Glue

Colored construction paper

Ruler

Here's what you do:

1 On colored paper, draw two 2-inch diameter circles, four 3-inch circles, and five 1-inch circles. Use a compass. Make all the circles the same color.

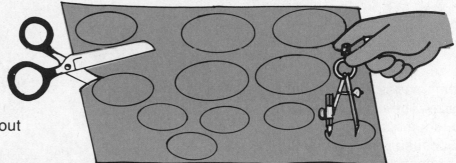

2 Carefully, cut out the circles.

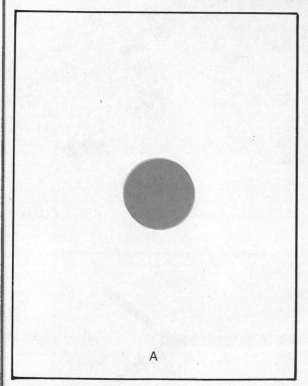

A

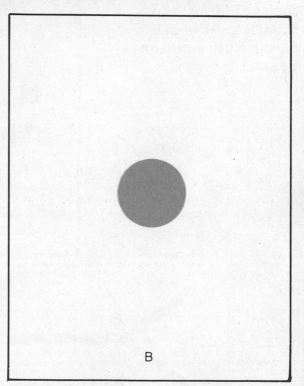

B

3 Glue a 2-inch circle to the center of a sheet of white paper. On another sheet of paper, do the same thing with the other 2-inch circle. Mark the first sheet A. Mark the second sheet B.

4 Glue the 3-inch circles around the circle on sheet A. Glue the 1-inch circles around the circle on sheet B. Look on the next two pages to see how to place the circles.

5 Now hold up both sheets and ask a friend which center circle is larger. Did you fool your friend? Did your eyes fool you?

The center circles on both pages are the same size. The circle on sheet A seems smaller because your eyes are comparing it to the larger circles. The circle on sheet B looks larger because it is surrounded by smaller circles.

A

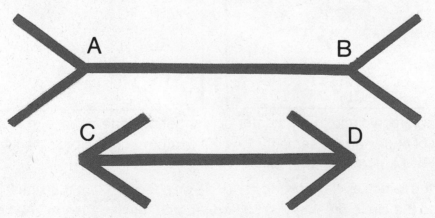

Which of these lines is longer — line AB or line CD?

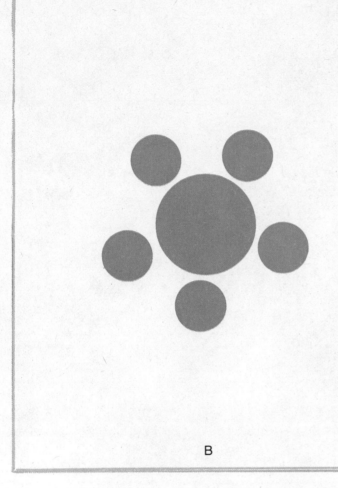

B

Is the hat wider or taller? Use a ruler to find the answer. Did your eyes fool you again?

WHICH IS THE PICTURE?

Is this a picture of a flower or of two people laughing? Which is the picture? Which is the empty space?

Do you see a flickering candle? Do you see
anything else? Look closely.

HIDDEN COLORS

Susan is standing next to her twin sister, Sandy. You can see that Susan's dress is green, but can you see the color of Sandy's dress? Are you sure? Try this experiment: Look at the belt on Susan's dress. Stare at it hard, while you count to twenty-five. Now look at the belt on Sandy's dress. What color does her dress seem to be? What color is her belt?

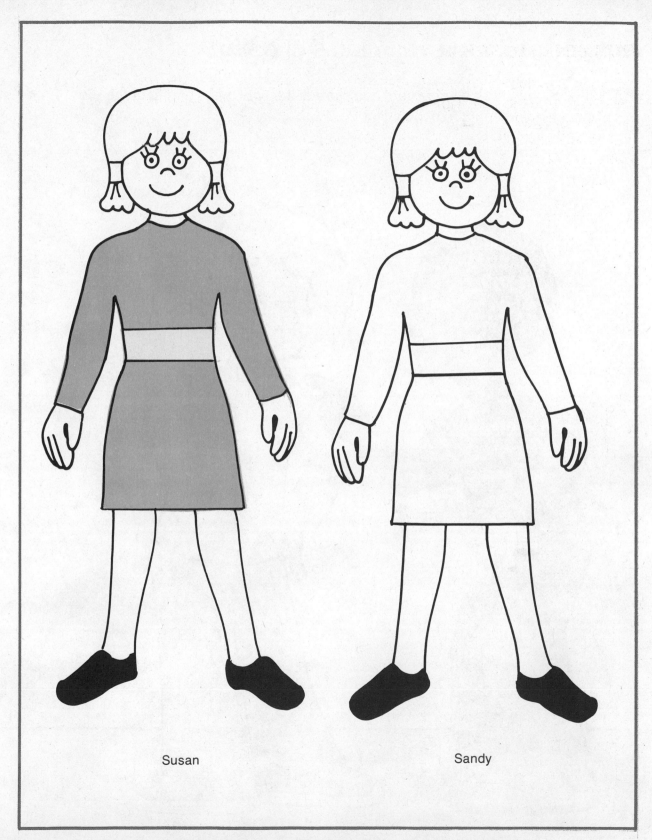

Susan

Sandy

CAN YOU SEE WITH YOUR EYES CLOSED?

1 Try this: Stand under a bright light and stare at the spot in the center of the heart, while you count to twenty-five.

2 Now close your eyes and wait a few seconds. You'll be surprised. You can see the heart with your eyes closed!

3 Ask a friend to try this experiment. Do you both see the same thing?

MINI-MAGNIFIER

Here's what you need:

Crayon

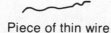
Piece of thin wire

Glass of water

Newspaper

Here's what you do:

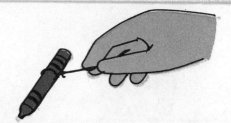

1 Twist one end of a piece of wire around a crayon to make a small loop. Take the crayon out of the loop.

2 Dip the loop into a glass of water. When you take the wire out of the glass, a drop of water will stay in the loop.

3 Carefully, so the water doesn't spill, hold the loop over a piece of newspaper.

4 The letters, seen through the water, look larger—the drop of water magnifies them.

UPSIDE-DOWNER

Here's what you need:

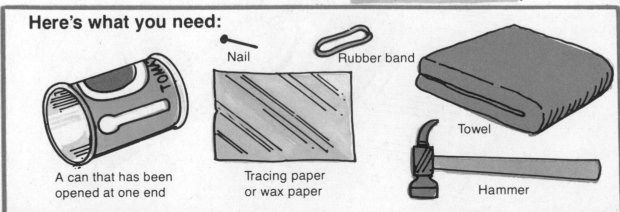

Nail

Rubber band

Towel

A can that has been opened at one end

Tracing paper or wax paper

Hammer

Here's what you do:

1 With a nail and hammer, poke a hole in the closed end of the can. Poke it right in the middle.

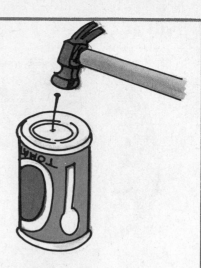

2 Cover the open end of the can with a piece of tracing paper or wax paper. Hold the paper in place with a rubber band.

3 Cover your head with a towel and hold the paper-covered end of the can up to your eyes. Let the end with the small hole stick out from the towel.

4 Look through the can at something very bright. Look at a flower on a sunny day. An upside-down image of the flower will appear on the tracing paper! Look at a lamp. Look at a candle. Everything will look upside-down!

5 If you like, you can decorate your Upside-downer with colored paper. Add some silver stars for a bit of sparkle.

(*Note:* You can also make an Upside-downer from a cardboard tube. Just cover one end of the tube with a circle of black paper. Hold the paper in place with tape, and poke a small hole in the center.)

HOW MANY BOXES? SEVEN OR EIGHT?

Eight boxes are right side up. Seven boxes are upside down. Do you see them all?

INSIDE OR OUTSIDE?

Is the bug on the outside of the glass tank or inside the tank?

COLOR SPINNER

You can blend colors with your eyes. Make a Color Spinner and see it happen.

Here's what you need:

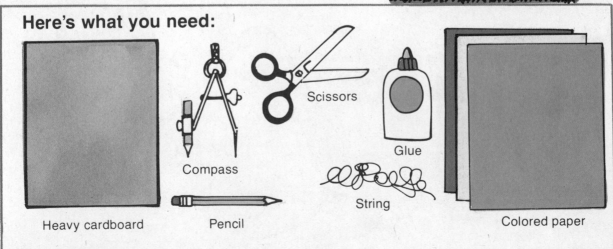

Heavy cardboard

Compass

Pencil

Scissors

Glue

String

Colored paper

Here's what you do:

1 With a compass, draw a circle on a piece of yellow paper. Draw another circle on blue paper and another circle on red paper. Make all three circles the same size.

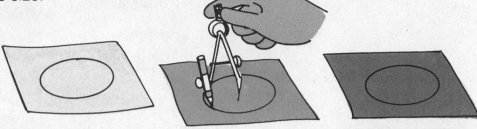

2 Cut out the three circles. Cut the red circle in half.

3 Glue the yellow circle to a piece of cardboard. Then, carefully, cut out the yellow circle.

4 Glue the blue circle to the other side of the cardboard. Then glue half of the red circle to the blue side and half to the yellow side.

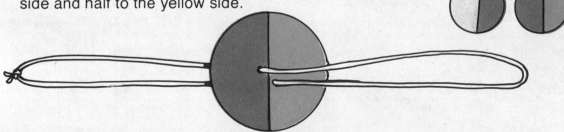

5 Poke two holes near the center of the circle. Push some string in one hole and out the other. Move the circle to the center of the string.

6 Hold the string in both hands and spin the circle by twirling the string.

7 When you have twirled it very tight, move your hands apart and together— as if you were playing an accordion.

8 Keep your eyes on the circle. What new color do you see? Look at the other side. What color appears there?

MAKE YOUR OWN MOVIE

When you see a movie, what you are really seeing are many still photos. These pictures are seen so quickly that your eyes blend them together, and the people in the photos seem to be moving.

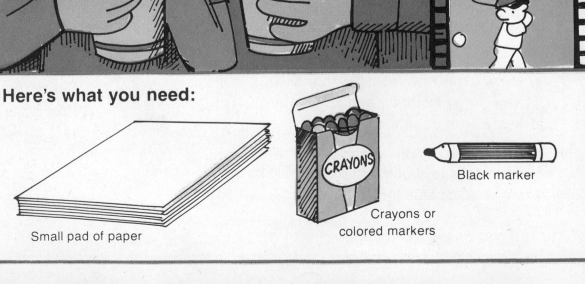

Here's what you need:

Small pad of paper

CRAYONS

Crayons or colored markers

Black marker

Here's what you do:

1 First, decide what you will show in your movie. For example, this one shows a boy eating an ice-cream pop.

2 Start with the page shown to the right. Draw the boy holding an ice-cream pop.

3 On all the other pages, keep the face and body in the same position. But on each new page, show the hand and arm holding the ice cream moving closer and closer to the boy's mouth. Note how the mouth starts to widen as the hand and ice cream get nearer.

4 After the ice-cream pop enters the mouth, the hand with the empty ice-cream stick comes out of the mouth and moves down.

5 You can watch your movie whenever you like by flipping the pages with your thumb.

6 You can add color to your drawings with crayons or colored markers.

WATCH THE BIRDIE

Can you get the bird back in the cage?

Here's how:

Hold this page in front of you. Keep looking at the space between the bird and cage, as you move the page closer to your nose. Watch the birdie fly into the cage!

A HOLE IN THE HAND

All you need is a cardboard tube —the kind you find inside a roll of paper towels.

Here's what you do:

1   Close your right eye.

2   Hold the cardboard tube up to your left eye.

3   Look through the tube at something across the room.

4   Place the edge of your right hand against the side of the tube.

5   Now open your right eye. It will seem that you are looking at the object through a hole in your hand!

WHAT DO YOU SEE?

Sometimes what we see has something to do with how we feel. Lots of people can look at the same picture, but they won't always see the same thing. Here's a game you can play called "What Do You See?"

Here's what you need:

White paper

Paint or ink

Writing paper and pencils

Here's what you do:

1 Fold a sheet of paper in half. Then open the paper and lay it flat.

2 Spill a few drops of paint or ink on one half of the paper. Spill some along the fold, too.

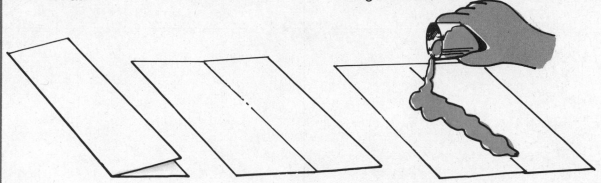

3 Fold the paper again. Run your hand along the fold and over the paper.

4 Open the paper and let the inkblots dry.

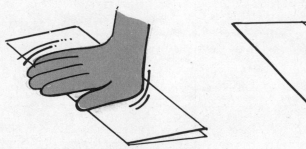

5 Pass out paper and pencils to your friends.

6 Let everyone look at the picture. Ask them "What do you see?"—but tell them not to answer out loud.

7 When everyone has seen the inkblot, ask them to write a story about what they saw. What is it? What is it doing? Use your imagination!

8 After the stories are done, read them aloud to one another. You'll be surprised at how many different ways there are to see the same picture.

On the next few pages there are some inkblots you may want to use.

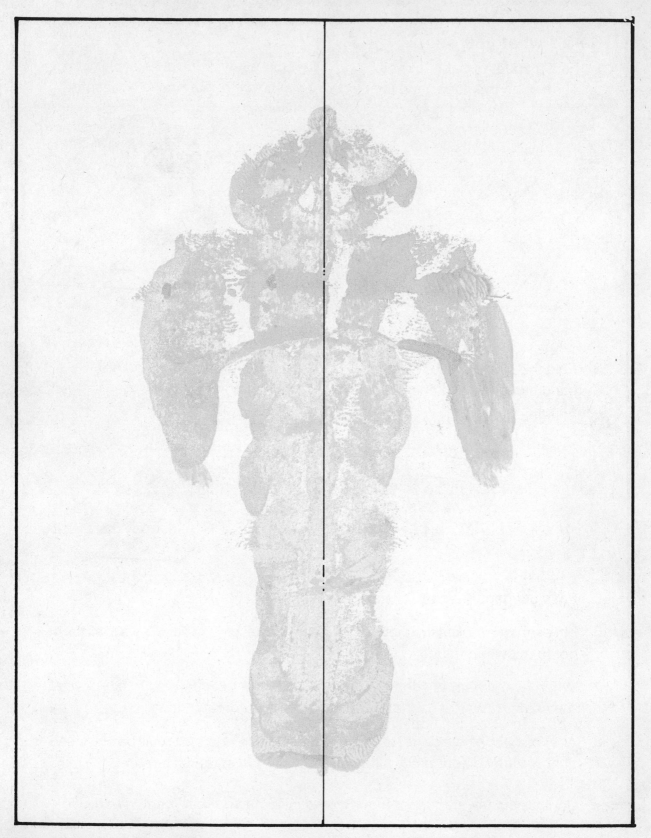

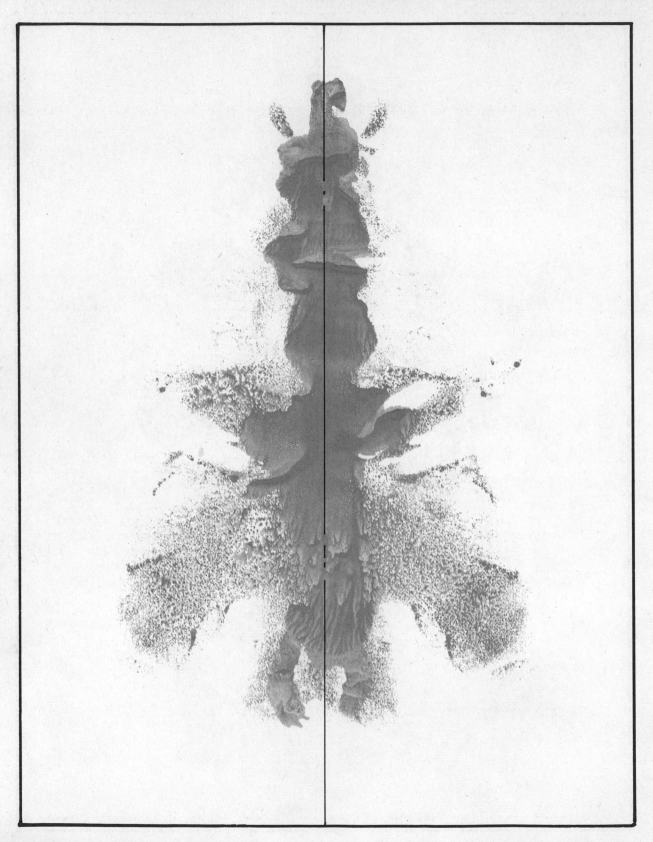

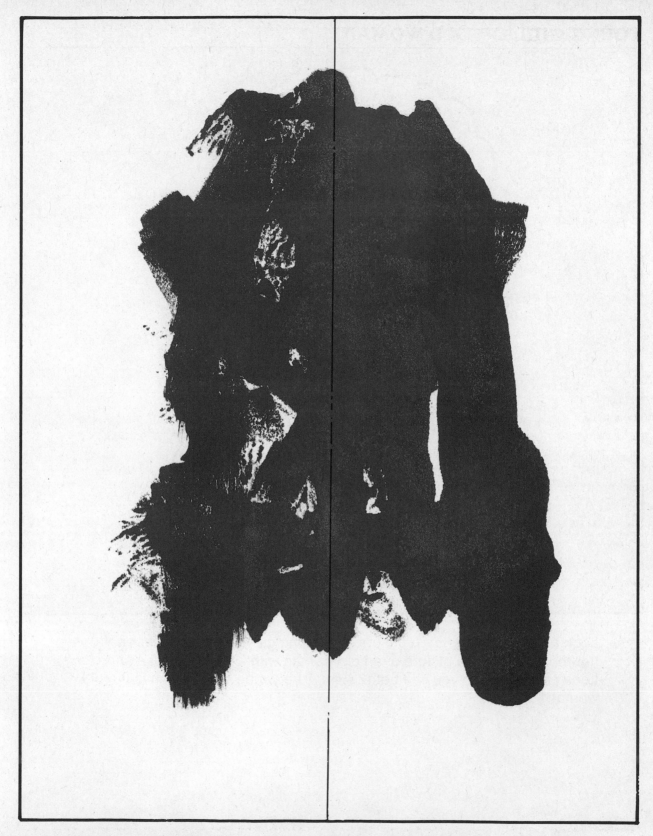

YOUNG GIRL OR OLD WOMAN?

Look at this drawing. Is it a picture of a young girl with a black ribbon around her throat? Or is it a picture of an old woman with a very big nose and chin? Look carefully. Can you see both? (*Hint:* The young girl's ribbon is the old woman's mouth.)

DUCK OR RABBIT?

Is this a drawing of a duck's head or is it a rabbit's head? Do you see both?

KALEIDOSCOPE

Here is an illusion caused by reflections of reflections.

Here's what you need:

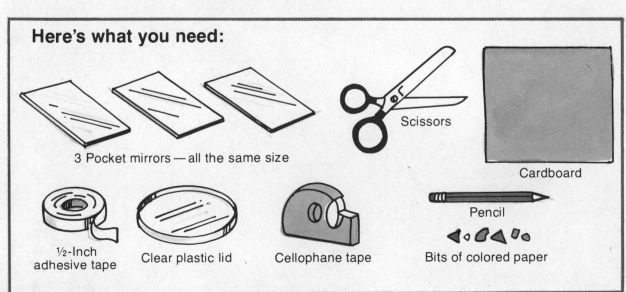

3 Pocket mirrors — all the same size

Scissors

Cardboard

½-Inch adhesive tape

Clear plastic lid

Cellophane tape

Pencil

Bits of colored paper

Here's what you do:

1 Stand three pocket mirrors so they form a triangle. Tape the sides together with adhesive tape.

2 Stand the mirrors on a clear plastic lid. Draw a triangle on the lid by tracing around the three mirrors. Cut out the triangle.

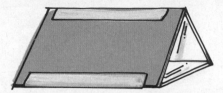

3 Attach the plastic triangle to one end of the kaleidoscope with cellophane tape.

4 Place the open end of the kaleidoscope on a piece of cardboard. Draw a triangle by tracing around it. Add tabs to the triangle as shown here. Cut out this shape.

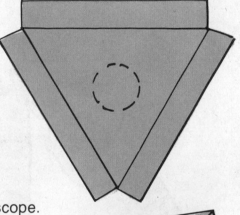

5 Draw a circle, about the size of a dime, in the center of the cardboard triangle. Carefully, cut out the circle. Tape a small piece of clear plastic over the hole. This is the peephole.

6 Drop bits of colored paper inside the kaleidoscope.

7 Fold down the tabs on the cardboard triangle. Tape the cardboard to the open end of the kaleidoscope.

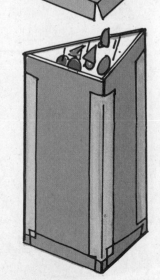

8 Look through the peephole. You will see the bits of paper reflected many times. They will fall into beautiful patterns. If you tap the bottom of the kaleidoscope, new designs will form. No two will ever be alike! If you like, decorate the kaleidoscope with scraps of colored paper.

SPINNING WHEELS

You'll see the tires on this truck spin, if you hold the picture in front of you while moving the book in small circles.

WHICH WAY, RIGHT OR LEFT?

Here's what you need:

3 x 5-Inch index card

Glass of water

Black marker

Here's what you do:

1 On a 3 x 5-inch index card, draw an arrow with a black marker.

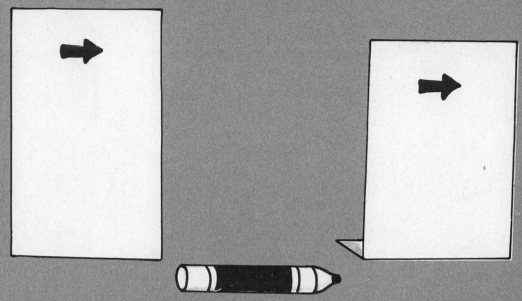

2 Fold the bottom edge of the index card so the card will stand up.

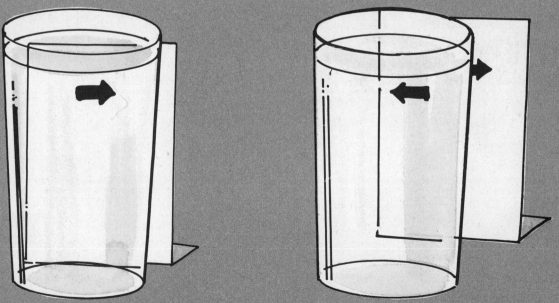

3 Put a glass of water right in front of the index card.

4 Now move the index card back a bit from the glass. Watch the arrow carefully. Which way does it point now?

HOW BIG IS SMALL?

To judge the size of an object we usually compare it to another object. Look at the opposite page. If you cover the pencil and the boy with paper, you'll find it hard to say how big or small the fish is.

Now cover the boy and look only at the fish and the pencil. The fish seems to be very small.

But if you cover the pencil and look at the boy and the fish together, the fish seems very large.

WHICH PUP IS BIGGER?

Can you tell which dog is bigger? Take a guess. Then measure them to find out.

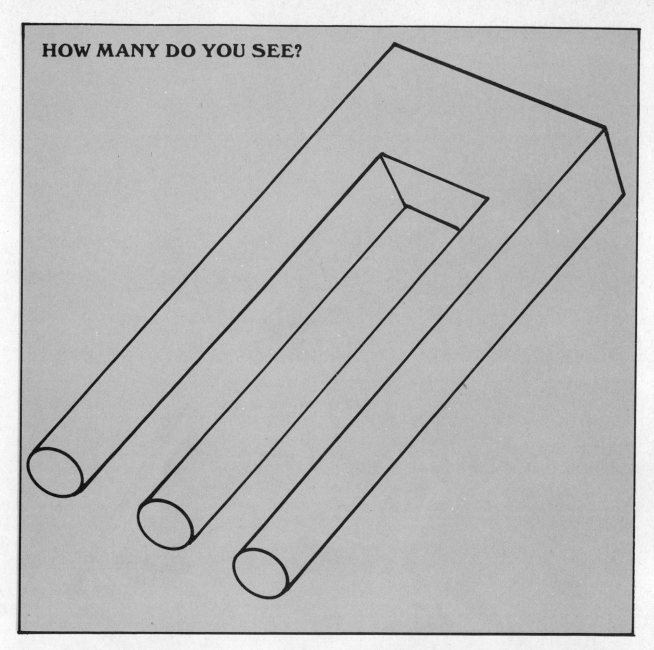

HOW MANY DO YOU SEE?

Here's a tricky illusion. Look quickly at this drawing. How many tubes do you see? Now look closely.

THE SECRET WORD

Can you read the word on the opposite page? Try holding the book up to your eyes on a sharp angle. Peer down the page.

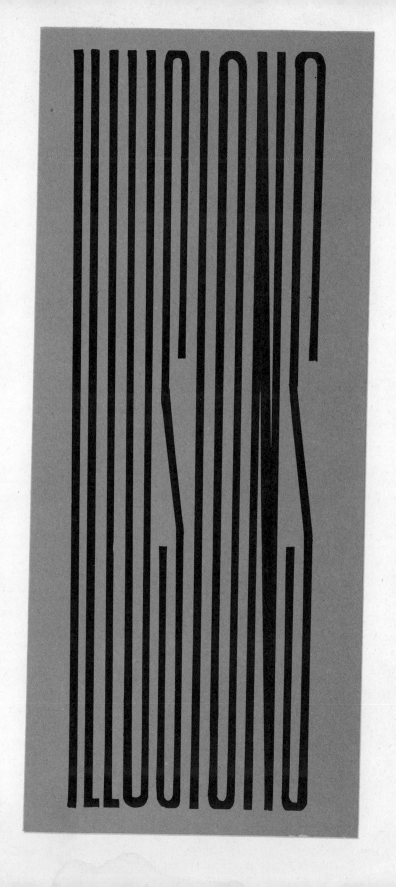